AF441019

Someone to Watch Over Me

Looking back on a life
of upheaval,
kindness & fortune

A Memoir by Sylvia Karwaser Goodman

Introduction & Dedication

My story is one of survival. But it also speaks to the immense power of generosity, humanity and good fortune along the way. Looking back over my journey so far, I know that I've been blessed with someone to watch over my every step. I have come close to injury and death far more times than I can recount. But somehow, my life was spared each time and my future made possible, albeit uncertain.

For this, and for all that I have and all that comes after me, I am grateful to the Almighty.

I am truly lucky to be alive. And I owe my greatest debt to a kind and generous couple, the Pontus', who took me into their home when all hope was lost. Their actions were invaluable to me and my parents, effectively breathing life into the next generation, and then the next. Thanks to their kindness, I am able to retell my story while millions of others perished, their narratives muted, their journeys truncated far too early.

Eternally grateful, my family and I dedicated much effort to tracking down the two people who took me in and saved my life. We wanted to ensure they were recognized for their humanity. I'm delighted that they are now honoured at Yad Vashem as Righteous Among the Nations, a recognition that will last forever.

I owe the Pontus' my life; I dedicate this memoir to their legacy.

Young Sylvia walking with her father,
Srul Karwaser, pre-war

Chapter 1

And So, It Begins

Both my parents began their lives in Poland. My father Srul (Israel) Karwaser was born in Warsaw on September 10, 1910 into a family of Chasidic Orthodox Jews. His father, Zeev Wolf, and mother, Ita (Yehudit), had seven children, two boys and five girls: my father, Elimelech, Leah, Rivka, Freeda, Bracha and Chana. Of these, only two survived: my father and one sister, Chana.

My father, the bon vivant

As a young man, my father was somewhat of a free spirit, always in search of new experiences and adventure. He was very handsome, debonair and had a beautiful voice. His love for singing and music, particularly cantorial tunes, inspired him to seek out the melodies that moved him.

It would also get him into trouble with his father. You see, my grandfather, an ultra-religious man, didn't believe music enhanced one's prayers. On the contrary, he felt it kept us from getting close to G-d. On that point, the son and father disagreed. Instead of joining his father at the Chassidic shtiebel (small, more casual synagogue), Srul would often head to the Great Synagogue of Warsaw – a popular choice among upper class worshipers looking for a progressive service.

It was there that he enjoyed listening to the renowned Cantor Gershon Sirota and the male choir. One Friday night, on the eve of Shabbat, my father made his way there again. As it was a far walk there and back, he returned late to the Sabbath meal and my grandfather refused to let him sit at the Shabbat table.

The old-fashioned ways of Poland felt constraining to my father's adventurous spirit. Besides, life was not easy for Jews living in Warsaw. With the war looming, anti-Semitic incidents on the rise, and a desire to seek a more modern life, my father left Poland in the early 1930s and immigrated to Brussels, Belgium to join his aunt and uncle, Tante Henele and Oncle Srul Kenigsman.

That decision to leave Warsaw would ensure my father's survival. Every member of his family who remained in Poland perished at the hands of the Nazis.

To be sure, Brussels was a more contemporary and stylish city than Warsaw. Hopeful that his move to Belgium would prove the beginning of a more exciting chapter in his life, my father immediately began to study leatherworks. At that time, most Belgian Jews were either in the diamond or leather trade, while many were also tailors.

Life was good – at least for a while. My dad had a number of good friends, was quickly developing skills for what would become a long and fulfilling career, and his love for music would lead to his discovery of opera, a passion he would enjoy for years to come.

My mother, the unassuming force

My mother, Chaya Gittel Higierowicz ("Getty"), was born on September 10, 1914 (yes she shared a birthday with my father!) in Wolbórz, Poland. She had a brother, Yidel. Her mother died when she was very young. Her father Michel, who worked as a tailor, remarried Branjdla Herschkowitz. Together they had six children: Helene, Israel, Jenta, Renee, Rachel and Charlotte. They all perished in the Holocaust.

The family of my mother's father eventually immigrated to London, England. Hoping to follow their lead, my grandfather got all the necessary papers in order. But, with the arrival of his new children, the documents expired. Thereafter, England refused to allow immigrants entry unless they paid a large sum for their entry papers. Instead, the family decided to move to Antwerp, Belgium.

Prior to their move, however, Getty was sent to London to live with her grandmother, aunt and uncle. Her father felt guilty about sending her away but believed it was the best thing for her.

She attended high school and was an excellent student. Though she wanted to go to college, my mother felt beholden to her family and familial obligations. So she studied dressmaking and soon excelled at her craft.

A few years after graduating from high school, my mother travelled to Antwerp to visit her family. It was an auspicious visit as my grandfather decided it was time to find her a shidduch (matchmaking for the purpose of marriage). My father, still living in Brussels at the time, travelled to Antwerp to meet this woman he had been hearing so much about.

With Yiddish their common language, the two proceeded to go on a few "dates", with my mother's stepmother accompanying them on each one. My father, ever the charmer, apparently made a strong impression. They quickly fell in love and became engaged after just a few meetings.

Higierowicz family in Antwerp, pre-war

Getty Karwaser with her uncle, Harry Hirsh
and a male cousin in post-war London

Getty & Srul Karwaser at their wedding

Chapter 2

A New Chapter

On August 10, 1936, my parents were married in a beautiful synagogue in London at a ceremony attended by all the relatives living there; unfortunately my mother's father and stepmother couldn't make the trip. The young couple settled in Brussels in a lovely home at 322 Chaussée d'Anvers.

My father had a workshop on the "mansarde" (also known as the attic) on the top floor of the house. By this time, he had already established himself as a talented leather bag designer, creating beautiful work and pieces for sale. My mother became pregnant a few years later. It was a difficult pregnancy and she gave birth to me on July 3, 1940. But the celebration was a muted one, marred by the realities of life at that time. To put it simply: being Jewish made life increasingly difficult in 1940 Brussels.

Let's not forget that Belgium declared itself neutral when World War II started. But that didn't stop Germany from invading on May 10, 1940. The Belgian military fought the invaders for 18 days before surrendering, leading to a German occupation that lasted until 1944.

In the 1930s, the Jewish population in Belgium numbered around 50,000. By 1940, it grew to approximately 70,000, with the majority of new immigrants arriving from Eastern Europe, fleeing the rise of anti-Semitism and other challenges that had befallen their homelands. Jews settled in various communities around the country, including Charleroi, Liège, Brussels and Antwerp (home to over half of the Jews in Belgium).

Though many Belgians fought against the German forces – both passively and forcefully – others chose to collaborate with them. It was because of those collaborations that the German army was able to establish two divisions of the Waffen-SS from within the country. Those efforts also helped make it possible for thousands of Jews to perish.

By the end of the war, more than 25,000 Jews were murdered, representing 44 percent of the total number of Jews living in Belgium at the start of German occupation.

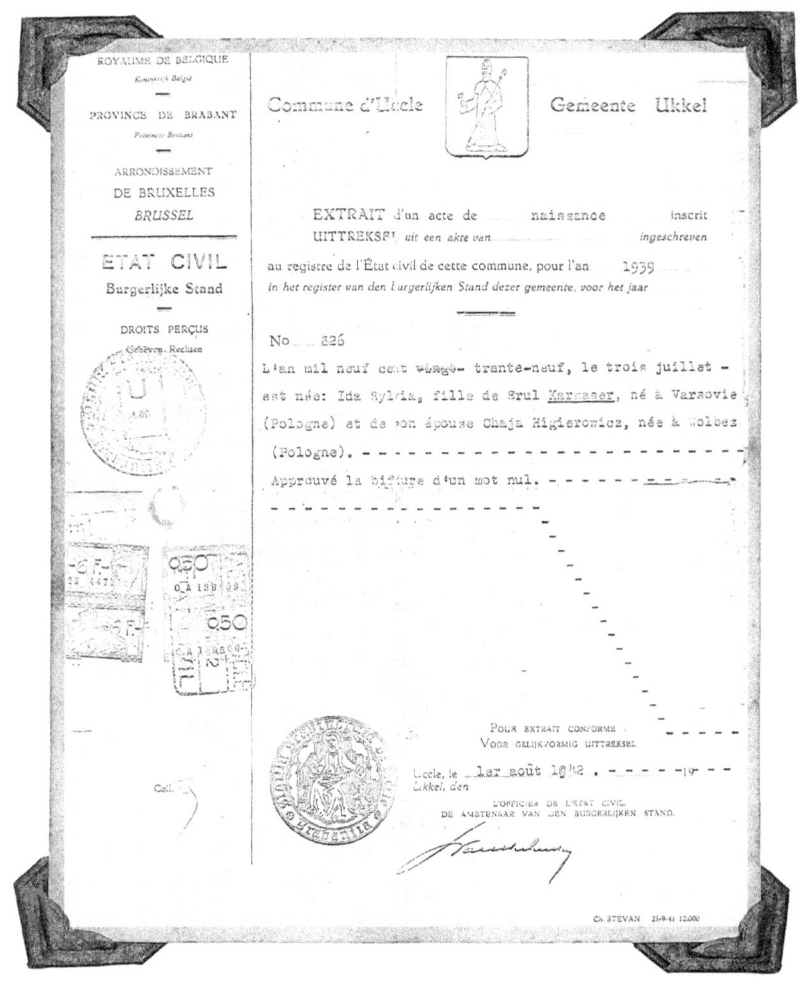

Sylvia Karwaser's birth certificate

*Front of the identity card "Stranger" that
Jews had to carry in Belgium during the war*

Chapter 3

The War Brings Change, Uncertainty

Life had been going well for my parents, but it all changed on that fateful day of May 10, 1940. A few months after the invasion of Belgium, the Germans passed several anti-Jewish laws. The Gestapo conducted raids on streets and in homes. They began to seize Jewish-owned businesses and forced Jews out of their positions; they were prohibited from working.

Jews were soon forced to register with the police station and the situation quickly escalated into an extremely dangerous one. Feeding one's family was now difficult, too. In fact, when I was two, my parents arranged for my date of birth on my official documents to be changed by a year older so that I would be eligible for rations cards (only available for children older than two years). That revision would remain with me for years to come, ensuring I was always one year older, at least according to my passport.

*Post-war memorial to the Jewish victims of
the Mechelen transit camp*

In April 1941, collaborators were responsible for destroying two synagogues and burning down the house of the chief rabbi in Antwerp during a pogrom. At this point, all Jews were required to join the Association des Juifs en Belgique ("Association of Jews in Belgium" or the "AJB"). Using the information found in the AJB registers, the Germans began deporting Jews to concentration camps in Poland.

Some Jews, like my mother's Antwerp-based family and my parents shortly afterward, were sent to the Mechelen transit camp, also referred to as Caserne Dossin à Malines, a converted army barracks that served as a collection centre. From there, the majority were deported by train to concentration camps, most to Auschwitz. In fact, between 1942 and 1944, 25,484 Jews and 352 Roma and Sinti were deported from the Dossin barracks, with just over five percent returning from Auschwitz-Birkenau.

By May 1942, all Jews had to wear the yellow star. My dad continued to work in his attic workshop, but my parents recognized the increasing dangers of getting caught. So they decided to conduct a little experiment. They asked one of my father's friends to question me about my father's whereabouts. The friend came to our apartment and asked me in Yiddish, "Poupée, vie iz dein tatte?" (sweetheart, where's your father?), to which I proudly replied, "Me meig de nisht zuggen az mein tatte arbeith die mansarde!" (I'm not supposed to say but my daddy works in the attic). Sure enough, the test affirmed their concerns. They needed to take extra precautions.

To add to their worries, children were in grave danger and faced little chance of survival as Germans deemed them of little value to their operations and objectives. Frightened parents, like my own, searched for ways to keep them safe. What were they going to do? As a parent I can certainly understand how incredibly horrible that realization must have been.

*The colour of this candy would ultimately
save Sylvia's life*

Chapter 4

The Distasteful Green Candy

By the end of the occupation, more than 40 percent of all Jews in Belgium were in hiding; many of them hidden by non-Jews. Some were helped by the organized resistance, like the Comité de Défense des Juifs (the "CDJ" or the "Committee of Jewish Defense"). Meanwhile, the Judenrat (Association of Jews in Belgium) started hiding Jewish children in convents, monasteries, farms and other places out of the watchful eye of the SS.

The group told my parents that they found a place to hide me – a small château on the other side of Brussels. The woman running the château demanded two years' payment in one lump sum. The place had been recommended by the Judenrat and my parents were desperate, so they obliged. The château owner also offered to take my parents' valuables - jewelry, silver, candlesticks, furs – and keep them safe. Obviously, if you could entrust someone with your child, you can give everything else away too. After the war we were able to retrieve some of those valuables, including a candelabra, and they remain in our family to this day.

At the age of two (technically three), I was the youngest of ten children brought to this hideaway. Consistent with the fashion at the time, the little girls wore dresses covered by an apron and the boys wore short pants and knee socks. Two weeks into my stay at the château, a stranger came by and chatted with the children. Upon leaving, he gave us each a candy as a parting gift. Mine was green. Since I didn't like the colour, I slipped the candy into the pocket of my little apron.

That aversion would prove my salvation.

The next day, all the children were dead, poisoned by the candy given to them by what turned out to be a member of the Nazi party. The proprietor of the château called all the parents with the horrible news, claiming total ignorance. The distraught parents were doubtful but there was not much that could be done.

*The Karwasers' candelabra that was saved
from the war used to light Shabbat candles
weekly by Rachel Goodman Aspler*

Photo of Sylvia with her father, Srul, which hung above her bed in the Pontus' home during the war.

Chapter 5

Desperate Times

After the incident at the château, I returned home to my frightened parents. What were they going to do now? How were they going to protect their only child? My mother was sitting at the kitchen table, crying, when our landlady Madame Pontus came to collect the rent. Seeing my mother in tears, she naturally asked her what had happened. When Madame Pontus heard the story, she was shocked and immediately offered to take me to the house she shared with her husband, and to pass me off as one of her grandchildren.

In truth, she had made a similar offer once before but my parents thought it would be too difficult for an older woman, who was already a grandmother, to care for a young child. But they were now desperate for a trusting hand to help them out. So they agreed wholeheartedly.

And how lucky was I to go there! Alida and Charles Pontus – aged 56 and 57 when I first moved in with them - lived on Avenue des 7 Bonniers in Forest, Brussels. They were kind, compassionate and saintly people who put their own lives in danger to save a Jewish child. I was fortunate to have spent two and a half years with the couple I referred to warmly as Bonne-Maman and Bon-Papa.

The safe home they offered could not have come at a better time.

Arrested and Imprisoned

On November 25, 1942, just a few days after I moved away, my father was taken by the Gestapo, and my mother would follow a few hours later. My father was travelling on a streetcar to visit a client when someone whistled the first few notes of Hatikvah. He turned his head toward the melody, looking to see who was singing. A few minutes later, my father was being led off the streetcar to Gestapo headquarters on Avenue Louise.

It was a setup. The intention was to encourage the Jews on the streetcar to reveal themselves. That my father was taken away was devastating enough. What made the situation even worse was the fact that the man who led him astray and later denounced him was a Jew. We would later learn that Icek Glogowski, or "Fat Jacques" as he was known, denounced many of his fellow Jews (rumour had it his own mother wasn't immune to his actions).

We will never know why he acted in this way, though one theory was that he thought his actions would keep him safe. Another suggested that, since his own family was deported by the Germans, he believed it unfair for any Jews to be free when his family was lost.

Despite many efforts to stop him, "Fat Jacques" continued snitching on fellow Jews until the end of the war. Though he was never found again, Glogowski was sentenced to death in absentia in 1947. When my daughters and I visited the Mechelen camp years later while on a trip to honour the Pontus' (more on that in a later chapter), a large picture of Glogowski hung on a wall in what is now a museum dedicated to preserving the legacy of the camp. I thought I was going to faint when I saw his face. Under the picture was inscribed the shameful past of a man whose actions will never be forgotten.

My father was forced to reveal to a Gestapo member where he lived and where his wife could be found. A short time later, the soldier arrived at our apartment while my mother was cooking barley soup. "What smells so delicious?" he asked, upon walking through the door. The SS officer made her serve him a bowl before he proceeded to destroy the treasured items found in the home. He even turned over a large travel bag that my father had manufactured and poured green ink over all the photographs stored inside.

It was common for the Germans to destroy or empty a house of its possessions upon arresting Jews. After my parents' arrest, Monsieur and Madame Pontus went to the apartment to see if they could salvage any of their belongings. They were able to find a photograph that had not been destroyed; it was a picture of my father and me. Bonne-Maman hung it lovingly on the wall above my crib. She also taught me a little prayer that I said before wishing my parents (one of whom watched over me) 'good night' every evening.

With the destruction complete, the German officer grabbed my mother and marched her off to the same Gestapo headquarters where my father and other Jewish prisoners were being held. They were detained for two days, offered neither food nor drink, before being shipped off to Mechelen.

Initially, upon arriving at the transit camp, my parents were added to the deportation list of transport XVIII to Auschwitz. Thanks to my father's superior leatherworking skills, however, they were removed from the list and transferred to the Werkleute group (the prisoner labour group in the Dossin barracks).

The camp was mostly populated with Jews, as well as some Romas and others; they were all put to work. My father became the head of the leather workshop and was able to "hire" some other prisoners to work with him, ensuring they also remained off the transport list.

My father helped others, too. One story relates how a Jewish prisoner entered a barbershop and proceeded to decry the Germans. Little did he know that a Jewish "Kapo" was sitting there, ready to denounce him. Realizing the danger, my father came up to the man and said, "If you say anything, I will kill you." My father was credited with saving his life.

Luckily, my mother was able to work with my father, using her sewing skills that she had studied after high school. She was particularly adept at her trade, having even sewed her own wedding dress (years later, she would sew mine too) among other clothing items.

As the head of the leatherworks department, my father enjoyed certain allowances that others did not share. He was allowed to leave the camp to buy provisions, for example. On a few of those occasions, he attempted to see me, asking the Pontus' to bring me to an agreed-upon meeting point. He was taking a huge risk, one made all the more dangerous by my inability to remain quiet, instead calling out eagerly when I saw him. Those meetings quickly came to an end to avoid putting any of us in further jeopardy.

My father found other ways to push the boundaries on those trips outside the camp. He would often steal potatoes, smuggling them into his overalls, before returning to Mechelen. He would then throw the potatoes into the bottom of the pot used to boil glue to make the leather they needed for their work. Upon cooking them, he would surreptitiously share the potatoes with others.

One day the commandant yelled to my father, "Karwaser!" and requested that he approach. My father was sure his life was over. But the officer hadn't witnessed the potato caper. He just wanted him to make a saddle for his horse. Never having done that before in his life, my father went to work creating a beautiful saddle from the leather he produced, an act that may have saved his life yet again.

Icek Glogowski, aka Jacques, who gave up
Srul Karwaser to the SS on the streetcar

Alida & Charles Pontus

Chapter 6

Life With Bonne-Maman and Bon-Papa

When I first arrived at my adopted home, I cried incessantly. With Yiddish my first language, I had a hard time communicating with the new faces around me. Besides, everything was just so different; it was a completely foreign world to this toddler. I eventually adjusted to my new life, though, in large part thanks to the wonderful and loving couple who did everything they could to make me feel at home.

Life during the war was exceedingly difficult and dangerous. Food was scarce; a good supper consisted of a bowl of oatmeal. There was a curfew of 7 p.m. and constant air raids that required us to head down to the coal cellar, which was pitch black because of the compulsory blackouts. To ease my anxiety, Bonne-Maman brought a doll and a little blanket into the cellar, which soothed me tremendously.

Over the next few years, I lived through some hair-raising experiences and narrow escapes. When I think back on those moments, I am reminded time and again how fortunate I was to have survived. Any one of those incidents could have ended my life or at least caused significant suffering. But I lived to tell the tales and, for that, I am grateful.

Despite these misadventures, it's important to note that I never felt abandoned by my parents. Though I was very young and my understanding of what was happening was limited, I somehow realized that my parents could not help it, that this was something beyond their control. I knew they loved me all the same and would be back to get me, one day.

In one event, a German soldier stopped to talk to my Bonne-Maman and her neighbour. He asked me a question in French and liked my answer. "Qu'elle est maline!" (How clever she is!), he said with a smile.

Thinking he was referring to the Mechelen transit camp (which some called "Malines", the French translation of the town), I quickly responded through tears, "Non, je ne veux pas aller à Malines!" (I don't want to be sent to Malines!).

Before the soldier had a chance to question my outburst, Bonne-Maman grabbed me and quickly walked away.

On another occasion, a neighbour was caught and denounced for listening to the BBC news on the radio, an illicit activity at the time. His actions led to a house-to-house raid on our street. I could have easily been found and taken away. Lucky for me and the Pontus', however, I had a playdate that day with a little girl in the neighbourhood. When the Gestapo searched the house, I was not there.

I also had a run-in with an older boy, a bully whose father was a "blackshirt", aka a Nazi collaborator. At that time, bread was not made with the white flour we're used to today. That flour had been requisitioned by the German army to feed their troops.

Instead, bread was made from all kinds of dried beans that were ground down and baked. The result was a very heavy bread which I could not digest. Always looking out for my best interests, my Bonne-Maman managed to get the local baker to bake one loaf of white bread that was set aside for me.

There I was sitting on the front porch eating my goûter, my white bread, when the neighborhood boy crossed the street and requested that I hand over my slice. I stubbornly (and perhaps foolishly) said no, at which point he kicked me in the stomach with his father's heavy boots.

This assault on my skinny young body was so powerful that it left me very sick for quite a few days.

In another incident, our backyard was bombed. It all happened so fast and, to this day, I am unsure as to how or why it occurred in our home. My adopted family and I were okay, thank G-d, but we were extremely shaken up. I was so scared, in fact, that I could not speak for a week.

Yet, the strangest, and possibly most dangerous, episode during that period of time was when my great-uncle Srul (from my father's side) took me with him on a visit to Malines. Family members were allowed to bring prisoners a few items, including letters. But this time he brought me, thinking it would give my parents pleasure to see me doing well.

The camp was far from my town, situated between Brussels and Antwerp. When we got there, there was a roll call for the inmates.

My great-uncle placed me high up on a shelf and told me not to say a word, not even if I saw my parents. When the inmates came into the room and my parents saw me (although I did not see them), they immediately thought I had been denounced.

In complete fear and fury, my mother was about to cry out but my father quickly stopped her, putting his hand over her mouth. Had she called out to me, her actions would have confirmed that the little girl on the shelf was a Jewish child. It would have been a devastating cry with significant consequences.

Sylvia with her uncle, Srul Kenigsman

*Sylvia with her baby dolls in a stroller in the
Pontus' garden.*

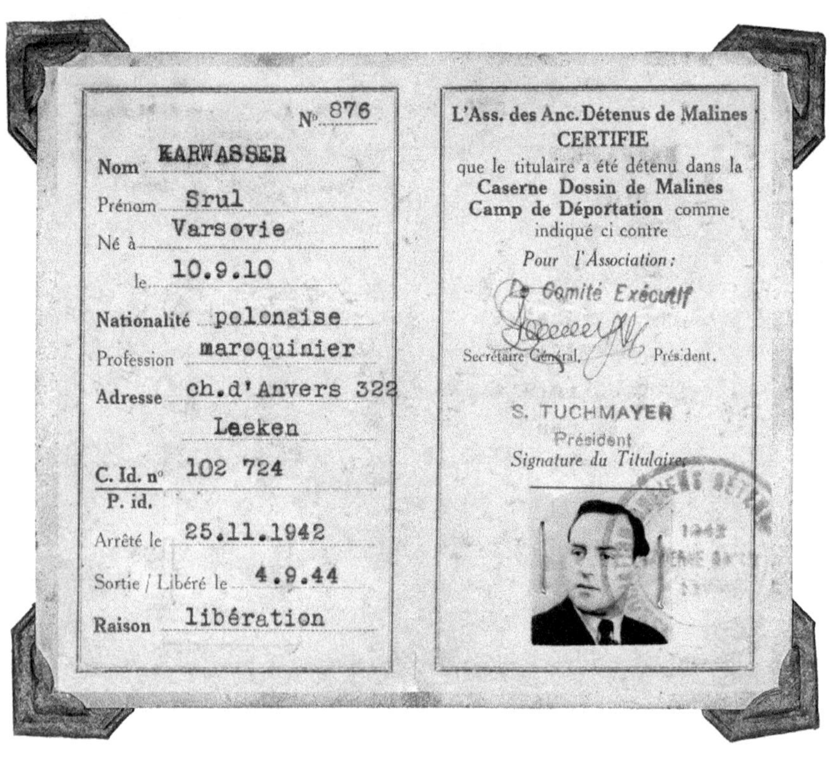

*Card given to Srul Karwaser upon liberation
from Mechelen camp*

Chapter 7

Liberation

On September 2, 1944, Allied troops crossed the Belgian border
at different locations and the liberation of Belgium began.
Within ten days, a majority of the country was in the hands
of the Allies. They captured Brussels on September 4, with the
Belgian government returning to power on September 8.

But the German occupation was not over. Two months later,
Hitler led his final offensive in the country with the Battle of the
Bulge. The liberation was finally complete on February 4, 1945,
when the remaining German troops left the country.

Shortly after the liberation, Bonne-Maman was bathing me
downstairs in the metal bathtub, a regular evening ritual. But
this time I wasn't behaving and had fallen back into the tub,
which made the exercise longer than usual. I was pushing my
luck, according to Bonne-Maman, who had often shared the tale
of the Sandman, a character who would throw sand in a child's
eyes if they didn't go to bed on time, without good reason.

It was 7 p.m. when the doorbell rang. I stood still in fear.
Obviously, the Sandman was here and I was in trouble. Bonne-
Maman reassured me that she would tell the Sandman I had
a good reason to be up, and urged me to see who was there. I
went up the stairs, my heart beating furiously, and opened the
door. Unbelievably, it was not the Sandman standing there; it
was my father!

"Papa!" I cried out. I then turned to the woman next to him
and exclaimed in confusion, "Who is that?" I had become
so accustomed to seeing the picture of my father that Bonne-
Maman affixed above my bed that I had no problem recognizing
him. But I had not seen my mother since I left our home
two-and-a-half years earlier, which is a very long time for a
young child. My outcry caused my poor mother to cry. When
everything made sense again, the three of us hugged and kissed,
so grateful to have survived the horrors of the Holocaust and to
be reunited once more.

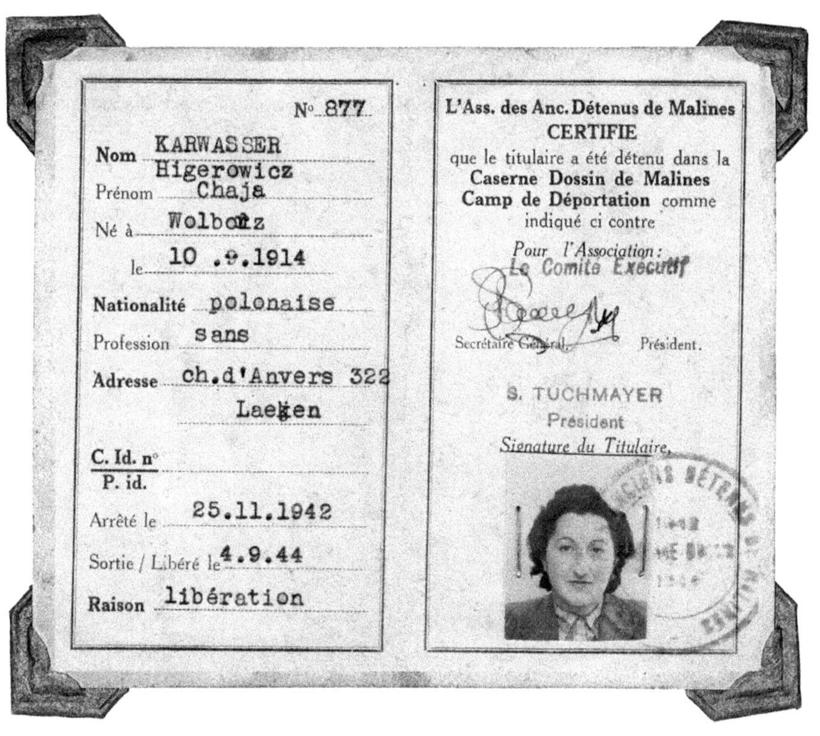

Card given to Chaya "Getty" Karwaser
upon liberation from Mechelen camp

*Karwasers at the seaside in
post-war Belgium*

Post-War Belgium: Picking up the pieces

Our first home after the war was on Rue Thiéfry in Schaerbeek, a municipality located in the northeastern part of the Brussels-Capital Region. My dad set up his workshop in the basement and quickly got his business up and running again.

Family reunites

I was attending a Jardin d'Enfants, a kindergarten, at a school fifteen minutes away. My dad would often have one of his young workers escort me there. Along the way, we had to cross a bridge under which trains would pass. One day, we noticed the wagons of the train were filled with freed prisoners and soldiers who were all waving and shouting. For some reason I thought they were waving specifically at me, not such a far-fetched notion for a young child.

When I got home later and my mother opened the door to greet me, I excitedly told her what I had witnessed, adding that Uncle Yidel (her brother) was one of the released prisoners waving at me! My mother burst out crying as she had not heard a word about her brother's fate since the start of the war.

As young as I was, I realized my comment had hurt her badly. A few weeks later, I again saw a train full of excited former prisoners and soldiers along the same route. But when my mother asked me if I had seen anyone waving at me this time, I recalled her painful reaction and immediately shook my head.

That's when she ushered me into the kitchen. Sitting there, still in his Auschwitz pajamas, soaking, and his poor feet covered with sores, was my uncle Yidel! He had survived! He and my mother were the sole survivors of the Higierowicz family. When we would eventually move to Canada, Yidel would follow a few months later before eventually moving to New York. We remained close.

Life resumes

Like other weary survivors, my parents focused on restarting their lives. They had another baby in 1946, a boy who they named Willy. His Hebrew name was Zeev Micha-el, after his two murdered grandfathers. My parents worked hard and business was good. My father soon acquired the exclusive Belgian rights to the plastic used for handbags and his business expanded significantly. We moved to a nicer neighbourhood and had a bonne, someone to help with the housework, etc.

We were moving forward. Still, old habits linger. While the Nazis may have departed the country, their anti-Semitic teachings were left behind.

I went to the local school from Grade 1 through Grade 6. In those days, the girls were in one building and the boys in another. I was a very good student and always received top marks. But the Directrice called me into her office one day and told me that even though I came in first among all the students in school, I was not going to receive the top prize at the annual ceremony. I would get the second prize instead. Why? Because I was Jewish. Oh, how I cried! And this after all that had happened during the war. The Germans had taught the Belgians well. But I learned to get over it. My parents told me I had done my very best, they knew it, and so did I. That would have to be good enough.

Time passed. Life went on. But we never forgot the couple who saved my life, who had given my parents the rare sense of security knowing their child was cared for and safe. Whenever possible, we spent time with Bonne-Maman and Bon-Papa. I used to visit them for Christmas and other occasions, and I have to admit, I loved the Christmas tree they set up and really enjoyed the holiday. In the summers our families spent time together at our home by the seaside; it was heavenly.

Time to emigrate

When I was in Grade 6, my parents decided it was time to leave Belgium. The Korean War that broke out in 1950 instilled in them a renewed sense of fear. People were already buying "the basics" in anticipation of shortages and an ever-growing concern that escalations may evolve into a Third World War.

My parents were determined to never go through another war. The only alternative was to leave.

The question was, where to go? My father first wrote to his sister, Chana Metzger, who was living in Haifa, to see if we could join her there. As much as she would have loved to be reunited with her sole surviving sibling, she recounted all the hardships facing many in Israel, and didn't encourage our emigration. My father was disappointed but he realized she was right. So, my parents looked elsewhere.

At that time, the United States was not accepting any new immigrants. The only countries open to newcomers at that time were Canada and Australia. With Canada situated so close to the U.S. and Australia in the middle of "nowhere", my parents decided Canada would be a better choice.

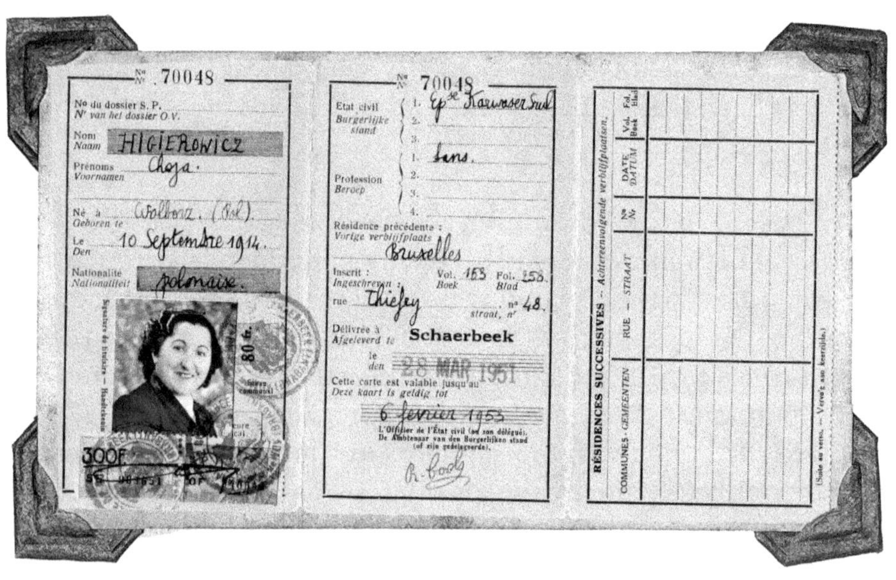

Getty Karwaser's identity card for travel to Canada

No
Nr .65600

No du dossier S. P.
Nr van het dossier O.V.

Nom
Naam
KARWASER

Prénoms
Voornamen
Srul

Né à
Geboren te
Varsovie

Le
Den
10. 9. 1910

Nationalité
Nationaliteit
polonaise

Signature du titulaire — Handteken

Sceau

80 fr.

100 F. 100 F. 100 20 F.

*Srul Karwaser's identity card for travel
to Canada*

L to R: Sylvia Karwaser, Getty Karwaser,
Michael Hirsh & Willy Karwaser

Chapter 9

Canada, Here We Come

In early July of 1951, we sailed for Canada. We headed for Toronto because my mother thought that an English-speaking place would be more liberal than a French Catholic one. We sold almost all our possessions, taking only a few precious pieces with us (e.g. Judaica and silver that had been hidden and not destroyed by the Nazis during the war).

We sailed from Antwerp to Dover, England. We spent some time with our family in London for a few days and then sailed onward from Dover to Halifax on the Scythia (Cunard Line). We had a wonderful crossing because we traveled first-class. As I was not yet twelve, I was able to travel on a child's ticket. It being a British vessel, everything on the Cunard was in English, but thankfully my mother spoke the language.

Two people were allowed in each cabin, so my mother and I shared one and my dad and Willy shared another. On the first morning of our voyage my father came to our cabin alone. Where was Willy? He was nowhere to be found. My mother called the captain, explained the situation, and the captain gave the alert: child missing! Everyone joined the frantic search for this five-year-old. They looked everywhere but could not find him. And then, suddenly, there was Willy. Apparently, he was bored waiting in the cabin, so he went to find the playroom where he had a great time playing with all the toys. You can imagine everyone's relief - especially my parents who considered Willy their miracle child after all the horrors of the Holocaust.

We landed in Halifax and then took a train to Toronto, arriving in the city's Union Station a couple of days later. We took a good look around; the train station was very impressive. Then my mother spoke to someone at the Traveler's Aid who gave us the address of a Jewish fraternity house at the University of Toronto. We took a cab to the accommodations.

Everything was new, everything was different; it was scary but exciting too. On the way to our new home, we stopped at a kosher restaurant on Spadina Avenue called The Quality Restaurant. What a treat for the first day in the city! The name, unfortunately, was a misnomer - we all got food poisoning!

Luckily, we were the only ones in the fraternity house since it was summer vacation on campus.

The next task was to find permanent housing. Thanks again to my mother's aptitude in English, we quickly rented a flat on Ossington Avenue, a few steps from Harbord Street in an area that had become popular among Jewish immigrants to Toronto.

In fact, adjusting to the new country was made all the easier for my parents thanks to the many "greenies" (term used for new immigrants, particularly from Eastern Europe) who became quick friends and with whom they shared stories and experiences.

The house had three rooms, a kitchen and a shared bathroom for two families. My parents set up the flat, bought beds, a kitchen table, a few chairs, etc. It was comfortable, it was convenient; it was home.

Life in Toronto

My father got a job in a leather bag factory, a difficult step for someone who had previously been a highly accomplished designer and entrepreneur running a successful business. But he learned to enjoy the work and the opportunities it offered our immigrant family. My mother stayed home to care for us and our new home.

That first summer, my brother had a freak accident that would forever impact his life. Returning from the corner store where he bought himself a treat, he heard someone call out to him. As he turned toward the commotion, a boy shot an arrow directly at him – and hit him in the eye! Thankfully, a surgeon was able to save his eye. But not only did he lose sight in that eye, the event affected him psychologically, too.

During my first two years in Toronto, my primary task was to learn English. The school boards didn't offer any "English as a second language" program at that time, so it was normal to set a student back a year or two until their English was strong enough to follow along in class. I was put back one grade, to Grade 6. Soon after, when I caught up, I skipped Grade 7 and was admitted to Grade 8 at Kent Junior High.

What a culture shock that place was! As was customary at the time, all the girls wore long skirts. But I wore only short skirts, as they did in Belgium. Girls in Toronto wore nylon tights; I wore knee socks. You can imagine how well I fit in. But I had two things going for me: I was a keen student and my mother had a new sewing machine. She made me these beautiful longer skirts and bought me some tights. I was on my way.

There were still other culture shocks to be endured, however. We had a homeroom teacher who would often leave the classroom (we later found out that he stashed his alcoholic drinks outside the class). With the teacher absent, one day before Christmas vacation a boy carrying mistletoe came up to my desk. I was unfamiliar with the custom and did not want him to kiss me, so

Srul Karwaser in Canada at his handbag business

I started to run around the classroom.

I kept running from the boy until I fell and broke my arm. The school called my mother and she took me to Mount Sinai Hospital. My parents couldn't believe how I could break my arm in the classroom. I lied and claimed that I got up to answer a question and tripped over a bag. I simply refused to tell them that I was being chased around by a boy who wanted to kiss me!

Great friends, great education

Because of what my family had been through, I always felt that I had to make up for their pain and struggle by being the best little girl and student possible. And I was. At Kent, I met my first best friend, Rivi Pekiles, who embraced a very different outlook on life than I did. In many ways, she "Canadianized" me and helped me adapt more easily to my new world.

After Kent, we attended high school at Harbord Collegiate Institute; it felt like arriving in heaven. I finally stopped feeling like an outsider. There were a lot of Jewish students there at that time, which meant we didn't miss any class on a Jewish holiday. Being at Harbord was amazing. It was there that I met my other very close friends, Hindy Petroff (Hirt), Ruth Kaplan (Zaretsky), Estelle Silverman (Grader), and Raymonde Goldgrab (Falko).

We went to the same summer camp, had some great adventures and even got part-time jobs together to help cover our expenses. We were a formidable presence! They called us the Big Four (including me, it's actually five but Rivi left for another school in grade 11) and we've remained close friends ever since.

As recent immigrants, my parents were more old-fashioned than those of my peers. The first time I went to a school dance, for example, my father insisted on accompanying me! I was mortified. But my father was good-looking and fun, and my friends enjoyed his company. He danced with me, he danced with them. And when we saw that the boys were against one wall at the gym and the girls were at the other, my father was reassured that we would be safe. I was able to go to the dance myself after that, as long as people walked me home - and they did.

My close friends and I belonged to a Zionist group, Hechalutz Hatzair, which was a great educational and social experience. We were privileged to have several great shlichim (emissaries) from Israel, like Aryeh Ben-Gurion, who had a real impact on us. In fact, Rivi went off to Israel for a year after graduating from high school (our parents didn't give the rest of us permission to go).

Once we were in high school, (there were 13 grades back then), you really had to study! I had a part-time job and was also very active in school activities, including sports, the orchestra, the choir, as head of the Girls' Club and president of other groups too. I was a high achiever, a go-getter, and always outgoing. But maintaining good marks was most important, as we all wanted to go to the University of Toronto. To my surprise, I was chosen to be valedictorian of our graduating class, which made me and my parents very proud.

Thanks to all my hard work and dedication, I did get accepted to my university of choice – the University of Toronto. I chose to go into modern languages, literature and philosophy. Initially I thought I'd be a doctor, but my mother suggested I volunteer first at a hospital to see how I enjoyed it. I was so squeamish, I went straight into literature. I did very well at university and in my fourth year, I graduated first in my program.

I headed next to the United States to study for my Masters in French Literature. I was accepted at all the top universities but didn't receive any scholarships. So when I got accepted to Ohio State in Columbus, Ohio with a teaching fellowship that could cover my costs for the year, that's where I decided to go.

I had an excellent academic year, but it was a fearful and contentious time in America. In the early 1960s, African Americans in cities across the country were feeling increasingly frustrated because of the high level of poverty in their communities. The frustration eventually led to a series of race riots in cities throughout the U.S in the mid-to-late 60s, including Birmingham, Alabama, New York City, Los Angeles, Chicago, and even Cincinnati, Ohio. Riots would eventually erupt in more than 110 U.S. cities on April 4, 1968, with the assassination of civil rights leader Martin Luther King Jr.

The violence made my father very nervous and he wanted me to return home immediately. But I stayed firm, assuring him I was safe in Columbus. Still, when one of my professors offered me a teaching position at the University of Southern Carolina for the following academic year, I decided to turn it down. Considering my parents' concern and the state of their health, I returned to Toronto after successfully completing my MA. In the back of my mind, though, I always hoped to pursue graduate studies in the U.S. at a later date. I never let go of that dream.

When I came home during the Spring Break, my mother had set up a number of job interviews for me with different high schools. The first one went very well – that is, until the principal asked me if my family attended the "Church on the Hill" on Bathurst Street, meaning Holy Blossom Temple. It was obviously not a good fit with my family's religious choices so I decided not to pursue that opportunity further.

My teaching career begins

The next interview was with Northview Collegiate on Finch Avenue. They had a large Jewish population at the time, and I was very impressed with the staff; I accepted the position. I was teased by friends who claimed that I wasn't hired because of my flawless French or high academic results, but due to the beautiful purple suit I wore for the interview that my mother had sewn for me. They said I looked like the kind of girl whose mother made good chopped liver!

I worked at Northview for three years and it was a wonderful experience. I learned a lot of pedagogy in that department and my colleagues became my very good friends. In fact, when I got married, my department Chair and good friend, Roy Jackman, gave the toast to the bride.

*Sylvia walking down the aisle at her wedding
to Osher Goodman*

Chapter 10

Along Comes Love

During my second year at Northview, I met my future husband, Osher Goodman. Though we shared some interests, we were actually very different people (opposites do attract!). He was more reserved, very intellectual, and was a wonderful bridge player (which I had no interest in!). Osher was also Canadian-born so some of his attitudes were different from mine.

He was privileged to have been born in Canada, and to have had a different upbringing than I did. He grew up in a modern Orthodox family, went to Associated Hebrew Schools (in those days it was an afternoon and Sunday school) and then studied at Yeshiva University High School in New York, leaving home at 15. He remained in New York to study for his Bachelor's degree at Yeshiva University and returned to Toronto for law school.

We were introduced by friends, Aviva and Ron Heller, who insisted he meet me. Six years my senior, Osher seriously pursued me right from the start. After six weeks, he proposed. I initially refused. Though I really liked him, I had those other plans. I still wanted to go back to the U.S. and start a PhD.

But Osher had a good sense of humour. He related how, if he ever lost a case in a lower court, he could always take it higher - to the Superior Court. "I'm taking this to a higher court," he told me, pointing upwards. He then made his argument: "Don't you enjoy spending time with me?" he asked. "Don't I take you to nice places?" He was very convincing. In fact, whenever I went out with other young men, my father would ask me how it went. I would answer, "He is not as smart as Osher," "He is not as interesting as Osher, etc."

Eventually I realized that Osher was going to win his case. We went to visit my friends, Hindy and Morry Hirt, and their new baby at Branson Hospital. After that visit, Osher asked me again to marry him and this time I said yes. When I phoned Hindy the next morning, she said, "You're engaged!" How did she know? Because I had let Osher hold my hand!

It was a quick engagement. We got married on June 30, 1965; I was almost 25. We honeymooned in Israel, the first time either of us had a chance to visit the country. It was a wonderful trip. We spent some time with my father's sister Chana and travelled around, taking in the sights.

We really enjoyed travelling. Over the years, Osher and I would visit many other destinations - France, Italy, Belgium, Austria, etc. We went on cruises in the winter and took other holidays in the summer. Of course, Israel was always a special destination for us.

It was understood that we would keep a strictly kosher home and that Shabbat would be observed. My parents were thrilled with the arrangement, as it was like coming home for them. In truth, I wasn't observant before I met Osher. But I valued harmony and believed that compromise was essential to any marriage.

I worked as a French teacher in Jewish schools for over 40 years and enjoyed it immensely. It wasn't always easy, but if you're good at what you do, it can be a very satisfying career. I always found creative projects to bring into my classrooms and enjoyed teaching my students about the beauty that is French Literature. I still have former students who stop me in the street. "Madame!" they yell, happy to see me, before relating a memory of something I taught them so long ago.

During that period, I also co-authored a series of high school textbooks on the French language. It was a busy and productive time. Beyond my professional work, I took every opportunity to share my experiences from the war. I spoke at synagogues, schools (including those attended by my children and grandchildren) and even my son's law firm, where many of the lawyers had never met a Holocaust survivor; their response was overwhelming.

Admittedly, I didn't initially want to talk about my painful past. But, as I grew older and heard about the rising anti-Semitism, I decided I better do my part. Though emotionally difficult, it soon became extremely important to me to educate students about the Holocaust, anti-Semitism and those who stood up to evil to help others. Like my parents before me who made every effort to share their stories, I believe the retelling is necessary to ensure we - and the following generations – never forget the past and our history.

My parents and I were survivors. We hadn't allowed Hitler to fulfill his goal. Coming to Canada was not easy but it has turned out to be an excellent country for immigrants, be they Jewish or from other religions or cultures. Although there were visible signs of anti-Semitism, like when I found out I had not been chosen for a top fellowship at grad school because I was Jewish, this still has been a great place to grow up and to start a family.

Sylvia & Osher Goodman wedding portrait
(June 1965)

Sylvia & Osher embracing with her parents looking on

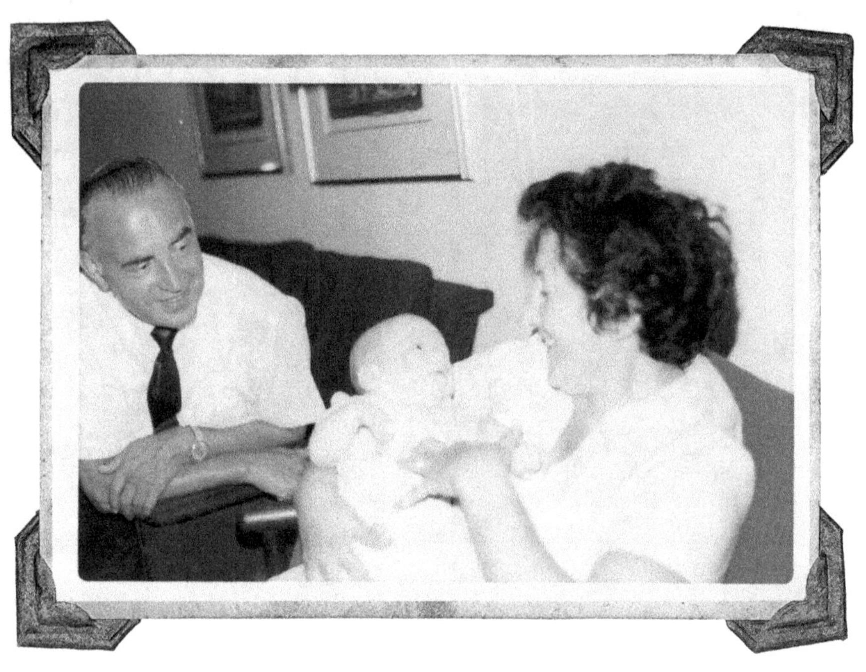

Getty & Srul Karwaser with their first grand-
child, Noam Goodman

Chapter 11

My Family,
My Joy

Osher and I had three wonderful children, Noam, Rachel, and Ayala, each of whom have brought great pride to my life thanks to their achievements and commitment to their Jewish roots and history.

Though I certainly played a part, I credit much of their devotion to Judaism to Osher. Ever since being sent to New York to continue his Jewish education, Osher developed a passion for community and Jewish studies.

He was intimately involved with Associated Day Schools and our local synagogue, which he attended regularly. And he was the "tutor" that all three of our children turned to when they needed help with a Hebrew or Jewish studies assignment. They embraced his dedication and integrated it into their own lives too.

When my daughter Rachel was ten years old, she won a provincial prize for a poem she wrote commemorating Remembrance Day, in which she included a reference to the death camps. She was interviewed on national television and made it into the Canadian Jewish News.

All three of my children received an excellent Jewish education at Associated Hebrew School, before continuing to CHAT and Ulpanat Orot. They were privileged to study in yeshivot and seminaries in Israel, Noam and Ayala for two years, and Rachel for one.

They all continued on to university too. Noam and Rachel followed their father's footsteps by attending Yeshiva University, while Ayala went to York University in Toronto.

They all have done well in their careers: Noam is a successful lawyer and trained Cantor (he inherited my father's musical talent); Ayala is a successful teacher at Associated Hebrew Schools and has a specialist diploma in special education; Rachel is a clinical psychologist.

When Rachel was studying for her doctorate, she learned about post-traumatic stress disorder (PTSD). Fascinated with the condition, she became involved with a specialized treatment program for Holocaust survivors and their families at Mount Sinai Hospital. Later, she was asked to participate in treating the trauma that many experienced as a result of September 11, 2001. To this day, PTSD is still a primary focus of her practice.

My children married wonderful spouses: Ayala married first, to Shimmy Wenner; they have two wonderful children: Elyanna and Ami. Rachel married Hudi Aspler from Montreal. They have three amazing kids: Nediva, Gavi and Talia. Noam married Elana Babb from Montreal and they have five terrific kids: Justin, Sierra, Jake, Zachary and Noah.

When my children were small, my parents used to tell them about their experiences during the Holocaust. But my father always tried to protect them from the horrors they witnessed by infusing the tales with a twist of humour or lighthearted remark. I have continued this tradition, adopting the same approach when sharing my experiences with my grandchildren.

I have been blessed to have such great children and grandchildren. And I am always mindful of the fact that it was because one Jewish child was hidden and saved from the Holocaust that there are now ten Jewish children going to Hebrew schools, observing Shabbat and learning to be good people. Hitler did not win this fight. It's important we remind ourselves and the world of that reality.

Though our children were always priority number one, Osher and I enjoyed our time together, whether traveling, attending classical concerts (our favourite choice of music) or the theater. After 38 years practicing law, Osher eventually retired in 1996.

A few years before his retirement he was diagnosed with Parkinson's disease, a degenerative disease that would slowly rob Osher of his ability to walk, talk and live independently. After a fall outside our apartment, it was decided that Osher could no longer live safely at home. He was placed at Baycrest, a long-term residence.

Each day, after work, I would visit him. We would sit together in his room and I would play classical music for him; Osher loved that. And I always remembered to bring his favourite treat: cherries. No matter the season, I would stop at the best fruit store in town to pick up the cherries before heading to Baycrest for my daily visit, visits that would last for eight years.

My husband suffered with Parkinson's for 19 years but the last few were especially difficult for him and exhausting for me. My work, my family, my talks on the Holocaust, each of those helped me get through it all. Osher died on November 9, 2012.

*L to R: Ayala, Noam, Rachel Goodman at a
family wedding*

*Family portrait of Sylvia & Osher Goodman
with their grandchildren, July 2008*

EXTRAIT DES REGISTRES DE LA POPULATION

MMUNE DE FOREST — concernant : FAMILLE PONTUS — Volume 55

demeurant : AVENUE DES 7 BONNIERS - 340 — Folio 181

N°	NOM DE FAMILLE	PRÉNOMS	NAISSANCE LIEU	NAISSANCE DATE	NATIONALITÉ	ÉTAT CIVIL	PROFESSION	OBSERVATIONS
1	PONTUS	Charles	S¹ Gilles	6/2/1885	Belge	marié	employé auf	1 marié à 2
2	de ROODE	Alida	Amsterdam	30/3/1886	"	marié	sans	
3	PONTUS	Adrienne	Etterbeek	16/12/1912	"	marié	employé	marié à 5
4	PONTUS	Madeleine	Etterbeek	23/10/1913	"	marié	employé	
5	Salmona	Isaac	Istamboul	15/02/1907	Turque	marié	bijoutier	marié à 3
6	SALMONA	Denise	Forest	24/04/1935	"	célibataire	sans	fille de 3 et 5
7	KARWASER	IDA	Uccle	03/07/1938	Polonaise	—	—	*

SALMONA, DENISE actuellement à Uccle rue GATTI DE GAMOND, 18 1180 Bruxelles

Pour extrait conforme :

Forest, le 17.03.03

Pour l'officier de l'État civil,
le fonctionnaire délégué

S. VANBEGIN

Census document showing the names of all the residents of the Pontus' home during the war, including Sylvia "Ida" Karwaser

Chapter 12

Recognition Well-Deserved

After visiting the Yad Vashem Holocaust museum in Jerusalem during our trip for my son Noam's bar mitzvah, I decided it was finally time to officially recognize my Bonne-Maman and Bon-Papa as Righteous Gentiles. Thanks to the help of my children, we were able to achieve this important milestone. But it wasn't easy.

For one thing, due to the formalities in Belgium at the time, we were not accustomed to using people's first names. As a young child hiding under a Christian identity, I referred to the Pontus' only as my grandparents. So all we had were their last names!

We reached out to my niece, Michal Freedhoff, who was working for a congressman in the U.S. who was well-connected. Sure enough, she spoke to someone in the Belgian Embassy and got hold of a 1942 census document listing all the people living in the Pontus household. Lo and behold, it listed the Pontus' first names: Alida and Charles.

We were surprised to see that, despite my being in hiding, the form listed me under my middle name, Ida, rather than Sylvia, as well as my real last name, Karwaser. We'll never know why, but we finally had the information we needed.

Remarkably, my daughter Rachel had named her first-born daughter Nediva, which means noble or generous in Hebrew, in honour of Madame Pontus. Imagine our surprise when we learned that Bonne-Maman's name "Alida" means the same in Dutch as Nediva does in Hebrew: noble and generous!

Next, we needed someone to corroborate my account of the story in order to affirm the recognition upon the couple who saved my life. But the Pontus' and their children were no longer alive, and we hadn't yet connected with their granddaughter.

A representative at Yad Vashem got in touch with Andrée Geulen-Herscovici, a non-Jewish teacher who was a member of the Belgian resistance. During the war, she joined the Jewish rescue organization Comité de Défense des Juifs and, over the course of two years, helped save almost 1,000 Jewish children by moving them into Christian families and monasteries. In 1989, Andrée was recognized as Righteous Among the Nations and in 2007 was granted honorary Israeli citizenship in a ceremony at Yad Vashem.

We weren't sure how Andrée could help us as we never imagined the Pontus' were involved with the resistance. In my mind, they were just wonderful people who volunteered to help my parents.

We were wrong. Apparently Andrée had an airtight bookkeeping system, whereby she recorded the names of Jewish children in hiding, assigning each with a code. In a separate book she wrote down the code numbers, along with their

Andrée Geulen-Herscovici

respective addresses. The books would never be seen together to ensure that identities were always guarded in strict confidence.

Andrée was more than happy to help. She wrote a testimony attesting to the fact that she had followed my story closely and checked in on me regularly. She affirmed that my code name was Irma Pontus and I was assigned the number 1639. Needless to say, I was shocked by her statement and felt even more grateful for all the people working behind the scenes to keep me safe.

What's more, she confirmed that the Pontus' treated me well, didn't take any money in exchange for their actions (another necessary criterion to be successfully recognized as Righteous Among the Nations) and were well-deserving of recognition.

With their names and Andrée's testimony in hand, we were finally allowed to pursue a formal request to honour the couple who saved my life. On May 16, 2006, Yad Vashem recognized Charles & Alida Pontus as Righteous Among the Nations.

Next up, the ceremony. When honourees are alive, the ceremony is performed at the Yad Vashem museum in Jerusalem. When they're not, it takes place at the Israeli Embassy in the country where the Righteous lived, in this case Brussels.

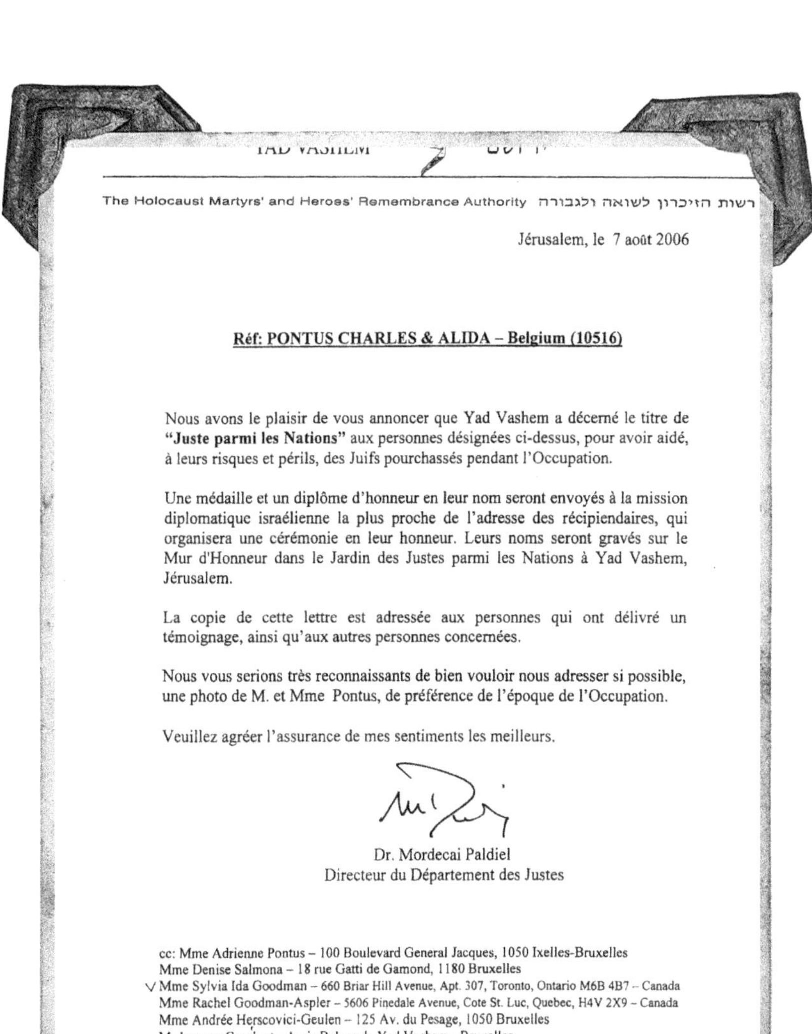

*The letter received from Yad Vashem recognizing Charles
& Alida Pontus as Righteous Among the Nations.*

*Diploma of Honour presented to Charles &
Alida Pontus by Yad Vashem, declaring them
Righteous Among the Nations*

Chapter 13

Off to Belgium

It was the first time I returned to my place of hiding since the war. Excited, my two daughters decided it was an occasion not to be missed. So, off to Belgium we went. It was a special opportunity for them to see where I spent some of the formative – and particularly impressionable - years of my childhood.

At this point I had connected with the Pontus' granddaughter, Denise Salmona, and she invited us to stay with her for a few days. We hadn't seen each other since our seaside holidays after the war. Needless to say, it was quite a reunion (and I was surprised when she told me her husband was Jewish).

On a cool November afternoon in 2006, with my daughters by my side, I watched as Denise and her daughter Alise accepted the honour on behalf of their grandparents and great grandparents.

Other attendees at the ceremony, held at the Israeli embassy, included Israeli ambassador Jehudi Kinar, the son of my parents' friends who survived Malines together, Henri Rabinowitz, as well as the Bainvol family, cousins who lived in Brussels. The ceremony was quite emotional. I spoke in French and my daughter Rachel delivered a speech in English and some French. Transcripts from each are found at the end of the book.

During our trip, we also visited Caserne Dossin, which houses a memorial and museum established within the former Mechelen transit camp. Of note, in 2012 the Memorial, Museum and Documentation Centre on Holocaust and Human Rights was established on the site, combining Holocaust and human rights education.

It was a very difficult day. Walking around Mechelen was not easy for me, but I knew it was important to my daughters and that made it worthwhile. Though both had attended March of the Living and were well-acquainted with stories from the Holocaust, this experience was personal; it really hit home.

Outside Caserne Dossin was a wall with a memorial plaque where we recited Yizkor (mourner's prayer) for all our relatives who were deported from there to Auschwitz.

As I mentioned earlier and as verified by the camp's register, my parents were meant to be transported to Auschwitz soon after arriving at the camp. Were it not for the fact that they were proven "useful", they certainly would have been.

Indeed, my parents were the lucky ones. Many weren't so fortunate. More than 27,000 Jews were interned in the camp. Around 25,000 Belgian Jews, travelling in 28 train convoys, the first one leaving August 4, 1942, were deported from Mechelen to Auschwitz-Birkenau. An estimated 1,200 made it back home. And less than one percent of the children 15 and under who resided in the Dossin barracks in Mechelen survived the war.

*Denise Salmona accepted the award by Yad Vashem
in memory of her grandparents, the Pontus',
with Sylvia*

After the ceremony, we stayed in Belgium for a few more days to spend time with my cousins, the Rabinovitzes and of course, Denise Salmona and her daughter. We took in some sights in Brussels before taking a train to Antwerp, where we spent a lovely Shabbat and weekend. We toured the area, visited two synagogues and then checked out where my mother's family had lived (Pelikanstrasse).

It was an unforgettable trip, more so even for my daughters than myself, who got to see up-close my birthplace and where their grandparents lived, the home where I was safely hidden under a new identity, and the camp where their grandparents were interned during the war. I believe the experience was profound and continues to have an impact on their lives.

Most recently, I'm very bothered by a growing level of bullying that goes on in our society. I speak about this topic a lot because it's one I'm passionate about as it has a strong relationship with the Holocaust.

What does that horrible event have to do with the bullying going on now, you ask? A lot! Remember: this is how the Nazis got started - bullying Jews and other groups.

Today, it's upsetting to see it happening to kids in schools, on playgrounds and everywhere. A bully is like a negative force; if someone is different, he does not belong, he can be terrorized.

We must do everything we can to stop it before it morphs into something worse, like anti-Semitism, which is already on the rise even in Canada. So, what can we do? Education is vital, but it's not enough.

We must remind people about what happened in Germany and to the Jews in Europe. As Pastor Martin Niemöller wrote in 1945:

First, they came for the socialists, and I did not speak out, because I was not a socialist.
Then they came for the trade unionists, and I did not speak out,

because I was not a trade unionist.

Then they came for the Jews, and I did not speak out, because I was not a Jew.

Then they came for me, and there was no one left to speak for me.

L to R: Rachel, Sylvia, Denise Salmona & her daughter, Alise, Ayala at the Yad Vashem ceremony

Sylvia Goodman at the Garden of the Righteous, pointing to the engraved names of Charles & Alida Pontus

Chapter 14

A Legacy Never to be Forgotten

My life has known much sorrow, pain and fear. But it has also been bolstered, time and again, by a multitude of blessings, good fortune and good people. I survived more near misses than I can count, and certainly more than I can fathom. My parents, despite their struggles, were lucky too. They should not have made it out of the transit camp alive, but they did.

As I mentioned in the speech I gave at the ceremony recognizing the Pontus' as Righteous Among the Nations, it is thanks to two outstanding people that I am able to write this memoir today.

It is due to their kindness and courage that my children and grandchildren have come into the world to share their lives with me. I cannot properly express the profound gratitude that my whole family feels toward Bonne-Maman and Bon-Papa. They not only gave me life, they gave me hope - hope for a better future and hope for humanity. They saved my life at a great risk to their own. Through their courage, they demonstrated that even amidst the pain, suffering and sheer villainy, goodness exists. And we must look to that goodness, always.

Let's not forget Anne Frank's quote from her famous diary, "In spite of everything, I still believe people are really good at heart."

And my favourite saying of all is from Le Petit Prince by Antoine Saint-Exupéry: "On ne voit bien qu'avec le coeur, l'essentiel est invisible pour les yeux." For those of you who were never in my French class, here is the translation: "One can only see what is important with the heart, the essential things in life are invisible to the eyes."

That is all for now, I did my best, and I hope it is enough.

Love,
Sylvia Karwaser Goodman, also known as Ma and Bubbie
Sylvie

*Sylvia with her children and grandchildren at
her 80th birthday celebration, May 2019*

My speech from the ceremony, translated into English:

For those who don't know me, I was a hidden child for more than two and a half years during the war. People often ask me how is it possible for you to remember all these experiences when you were so little? I understand their surprise and I know that my own children don't have many memories of their very first years.

Thank G-d they don't have the same type of memories I had to suffer so young. It was really traumatic to be separated from my parents. At that time, my parents were renting an apartment from the Pontus couple. Mme. Pontus had already offered to take me, but my parents thought it would be too hard for her.

I was therefore placed in a large home chosen by the Judenrat. What a disaster! The woman denounced her charges (there were approximately eight or ten) to the Gestapo. So after being the only child alive after a horrible episode, I returned to my family.

When my Bonne-Maman came to collect the rent, my mother was crying having just found out that her family from Antwerp had been caught by the Nazis and sent off to Caserne Dossin on the way to Auschwitz. Mme. Pontus swore to my parents that she would treat me like one of her own grandchildren, which she did, and much more.

Being separated from my parents was difficult at first, since at that point I spoke more Yiddish than French. But I got used to it very quickly. And one week later, my parents were caught and sent to Malines (Caserne Dossin).

Bonne-Maman and Bon-Papa did everything possible to make this very difficult situation as normal as possible. For example, when there was an air raid or a bombing on the street, we had to go down to the coal cellar, and a little blanket and a dolly awaited me there! The war bread was very heavy and I couldn't digest it, so Bonne-Maman traded some of our previous food stamps so that the baker baked one loaf of white bread — only for me!

My Bonne-Maman had gone back to my parents' apartment to see if there was anything left to salvage; nothing was left except for some pictures on which the Nazis had spilled some green ink. She looked through all the pictures and found one without ink splashed all over it of my daddy, and she took this picture and hung it over my bed and every night we recited a prayer, asking G-d to keep everyone safe.

I knew that my parents loved me and that it was not their fault. I had not been abandoned. Thanks to the love showered on me, helped me be a "normal" little girl and playful during these very difficult times.

My parents were interned in Caserne Dossin in Malines. They were supposed to be on the next convoy to Auschwitz when they were liberated and we were reunited at the Pontus's home. After the war until our immigration to Canada, I spent wonderful times with my "grandparents" the Pontus'. Monsieur Pontus died in 1950 and Madame Pontus in 1951, when we were already in Canada.

Unfortunately, we lost contact with the rest of the family. However, we never ever forgot the great risk my Bonne-Maman and Bon-Papa took by hiding me in their home. It is thanks to my daughter Rachel and her research that we were finally able to have the Pontus family recognized by Yad Vashem.

My entire family knows that it is thanks to the courage and goodness of Alida and Charles Pontus that I survived and that my parents survived and thus were able to fool Hitler.

"On ne voit bien qu'avec le Coeur; L'essential est invisible pour les yeux." Alida and Charles Pontus saw with their hearts what was essential in life; save it, preserve it and appreciate. I try never to forget this important lesson.

My daughter Rachel Goodman Aspler's speech from the ceremony:

Here I am today, humbled to have the honour of addressing the guests, especially the Pontus family. It seems to my sister Ayala and myself that we have been waiting all our lives for this moment. From our earliest childhood, our grandparents and our mother used to tell us how the Pontus family had saved our mother during the Holocaust. Not only had they hidden her in their home for more than two long years, they also treated her like a member of the family, where not only did she feel safe but also well-loved.

Our grandparents, Srul and Getty Karwasser, may Hashem [....], often spoke of their experiences during the war. Naturally, all that had a real impact on our youth. Being the child and grandchild of a survivor of the Shoah always played a major role in the development of our identities.

We were truly interested in the literature of the Holocaust and participated in commemorative assemblies at school and in the Jewish community. Ayala and I participated in the March of the Living. Not only did we visit the concentration camps but also saw what the Jewish world had lost because of the Shoah. Personally, I specialized in psychology and wrote my doctoral thesis on the trauma suffered even to this day by survivors and even some of their children.

In spite of all this, it always seemed to me that there was something [missing] in our lives: having Alida and Charles Pontus recognized for their heroism. Thus, a few years ago, the long quest to have them recognized as Righteous Among the Nations at Yad Vashem. One of the obligations of Judaism is called, "Hakarat Hatov," which means recognizing the goodness of people.

It is not always easy to show our gratitude because this act underlines our dependence on others. However, we are encouraged to overcome this emotion in order to recall where we came from. We honour those who do good in order to encourage others to follow their example. In a world where many people when speaking of the Holocaust still say, "Nothing more could have been done to save the Jews," the heroism of the Pontus couple prove that this expression is obviously false.

Now that we can finally realize our obligation, I represent our entire family when I say that there are no words to express how grateful we are for the heroism of the Pontus couple. Without their altruistic behaviour, which placed their own lives in danger, it is certain that our mother, her parents, us children and our own children would not be of this world.

Therefore, because of their great hearts and the heroism of Alida and Charles Pontus, our two families will always be linked. That is why when my first child was born in 2002, my husband and I named her Nediva, which means "noble and generous" in honour of Mme. Pontus, whom our mother called Bonne-Maman.

When our daughter was born, we hadn't yet discovered the first names of the Pontus couple. And it's only by chance that we finally discovered their first names as well as all the occupants of the family during the war. It showed the first names of the Pontus couple. Bonne-Maman's first name, Alida, by miracle in Dutch also means "noble and generous", like the name we chose to honour Bonne-Maman for our daughter Nediva! God acts in mysterious ways, n'est-ce pas? I hope and pray that our grandparents are watching from above and smiling at the circle of our obligation.

Personally, and on behalf of our entire family, I promise to live life to the fullest but mainly to follow the example of Alida and Charles Pontus, to choose altruism instead of egoism, courage instead of fear and love towards humanity instead of hate. Thank you.

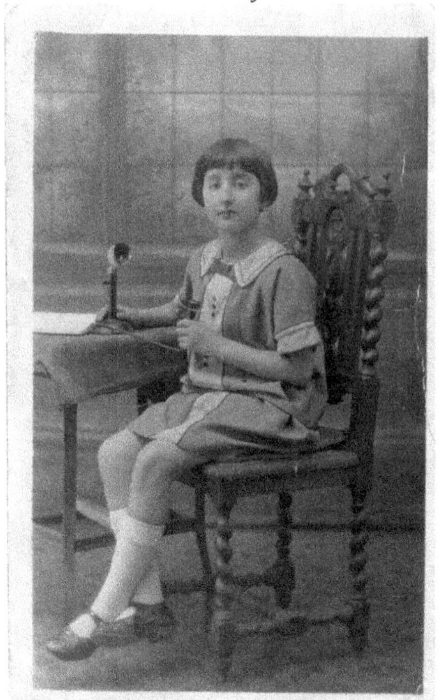

Chaya (Getty) Higierowicz as
young girl

Sylvia & Willy Karwaser at the beach,
post-war Belgium

Willy Karwaser, passport photo

Denise Salmona (Pontus' granddaughter) and
Sylvia in post-war Belgium

Sylvia Karwaser as a girl in post-war
Belgium

Srul Karwaser, passport photo

Willy Karwaser Bar Mitzvah portrait
(February 1959)

Getty Karwaser, passport photo

Sylvia with her friends at Camp Kvutza

Group photo of Sylvia & friends at Camp
Kvutza

Sylvia Karwaser, portrait

Sylvia with her father, Srul

Sylvia Goodman, wedding photo

Sylvia & Osher Goodman wedding photo with Uncle
Srul & Tante Henele Kenigsman (June 1965)

David Goodman with Osher & Sylvia Goodman

Sylvia Karwaser, portrait

Getty & Srul Karwaser

Srul Karwaser with his sister, Chana Metzger and her grandchildren, in Israel

L to R: Sylvia & Osher Goodman, Sholom & Ethel Goodman, Stephen & Helen Freedhoff, Doba & David Goodman

Sylvia & Osher Goodman on vacation

Sylvia Karwaser, portrait

L to R: Hindy Hirt, Sylvia Goodman,
Ruth Zaretsky, Rivi Ullmann at Noam's
Bar Mitzvah party (June 1982)

Srul & Getty Karwaser

Getty & Srul Karwaser

Top to Bottom: Chana Metzger (Srul's sister) with
her daughter, Ruti Tauber, Rachel Goodman in
centre, surrounded by Ruti's children

Sylvia & Osher Goodman

Noam Goodman reading the Torah at the Kotel at his Bar Mitzvah in Israel (July 1982)

Sylvia with daughters, Rachel & Ayala, at Noam's Bar Mitzvah celebration, in dresses sewn by Getty Karwaser

L to R back row: Srul & Getty Karwaser, Sylvia & Osher Goodman, Noam, Ethel & Sholom Goodman Front row: Rachel & Ayala, at the awards ceremony for Rachel winning the poetry contest (1983)

```
                MY  POPPY


      I am proud to wear a poppy,

      In rememberance of all those men and women

      Who fought so bravely,

      To save all the elderly and the children.


      I wear it for the unfortunate,

      Whose parents did not return.

      And for all those grieving people,

      In whose souls only memories burn.


      For all the ones who were slaughtered

      And the ones who were slaves,

      For the ones in the camps,

      For all those long, hard days.


      We try to remember,

      We try to recall.

      We all want to see them,

      But they are not coming back, never at all.


      I am proud to wear my poppy,

      And it makes me think these thoughts.

      Of all the courageous soldiers,

      Who died because they fought.

                              Rachel Goodman
```

Rachel Goodman's winning poem (1983)

Rachel Goodman, 11, of the Associated Hebrew Schools, won first place in the junior category (grades 4, 5 and 6) in all levels — branch, district, zone and province — of the Royal Canadian Legion Remembrance Day Poem Contest. At an assembly in the school's Neptune branch, Rachel was presented with the Legion's provincial gold medal and certificate by George McEachran (right), district chairman, youth education committee, Royal Canadian Legion District D. With them is Rabbi Akiva Egozi, the school's educational director. (Ben Lechtman photo)

CJN article on Rachel Goodman winning poetry contest (1983)

Noam Goodman's graduation
photo from Osgoode Law School
(June 1994)

Getty Karwaser surrounded by her children, Sylvia
& Willy, at the wedding of Ayala & Shimmy Wenner
(November 1995)

Osher & Sylvia Goodman
walking down the aisle at Ayala's
wedding (November 1995)

L to R: Ayala Wenner, Getty Karwaser, Rachel
Goodman, Ethel Goodman at Ayala's wedding
(November 1995)

Sylvia & Osher Goodman with their first
grandchild, Elyanna Wenner

Wedding of Ayala & Shimmy Wenner
(November 1995)

L to R: Aviva Heller, Sylvia Goodman, Hindy Hirt at
Ayala & Shimmy Wenner's wedding (November 1995)

Ayala Wenner York University B.A.
and B.Ed graduation photo
(June 1997)

L to R: Noam Goodman, Sylvia & Osher Goodman,
Rachel Goodman

Rachel Goodman receiving
her Doctoral degree in Clinical
Psychology from St. John's University
in New York (May 2000)

Wedding of Rachel & Hudi Aspler (May 2001)

L to R: Ethel Goodman, Sylvia
Goodman, Helen Freedhoff, Rachel
Goodman Aspler at Rachel & Hudi's
wedding (May 2001)

Wedding of Noam & Elana Goodman
(August 2001)

L to R: Hindy Hirt, Ruth Zaretsky, Mory Hirt, Sylvia
Goodman on a hike

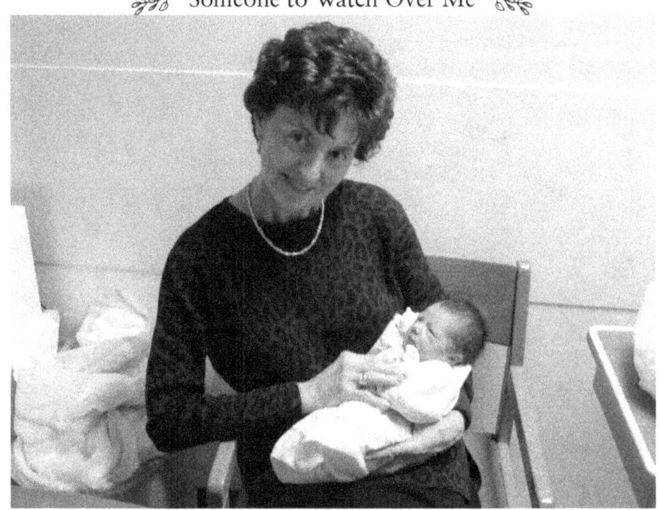

Sylvia with baby, Nediva Aspler, who is named in
memory of Alida Pontus (December 2002)

Top to Bottom: Ayala Wenner, Sylvia Goodman,
Rachel Goodman Aspler, cousins from Belgium
after the Yad Vashem ceremony

L to R: Helen Freedhoff, Sylvia Goodman,
Doba Goodman, Hindy Hirt

Osher & Sylvia Goodman

Sylvia with Ruth & Oscar Zaretsky & Hindy
Hirt on vacation at Lake Louise

January 25, 2007 — The Canadian Jewish News — Page 27

Coast to Coast

Brussels ceremony recalls couple who hid toddler

By DAVID LAZARUS
Staff Reporter

Sylvia Karwaser was only two years old in 1942 when Alida Pontus and her husband, Charles, both non-Jews and getting on in years, saved the very young girl's life by sheltering her from the Nazis in their own home in Brussels for more than two years.

Yet according to Karwaser's daughter, Rachel Goodman-Aspler of Montreal, her mother, a longtime educator at the Community Hebrew Academy of Toronto whose married name is Sylvia Goodman and is now 66, still retains faint memories from that time.

Those recollections were stirred anew, Goodman-Aspler said, at a moving November ceremony in Brussels to bestow Yad Vashem's "Righteous Among the Nations" honour upon the couple, who are now deceased.

The honour was accepted at the Israeli Embassy in Brussels by the Pontuses' granddaughter, Denise Salmona, and great-granddaughter, Alise. Also in attendance were Goodman-Aspler, her mother, sister Ayala, Yad Vashem officials, and Israeli ambassador Jehudi Kinar.

"It took a long time, because we never knew the Pontuses' first names," Goodman-Aspler said in an interview. "We had had the family name and addresses, but nothing else. [Alida Pontus] was always referred to as 'bonne maman.'"

The ceremony was the culmination of a dogged effort by Goodman-Aspler and others dating back more than a decade to have Yad Vashem give the Pontuses their due.

But the application could not be properly completed until all the pertinent information – including the Pontuses' first names and at least one person to corroborate what they did – could be supplied to Yad Vashem. Sylvia was too young to really remember or vouch for the couple that saved her.

"I'm here today because of that family," Goodman-Aspler said. "They deserved to be recognized."

In 1942 Brussels, two years after the Nazis occupied Belgium, Sylvia Karwaser was living in an apartment building with her parents, Srul and Chaya (Goodman-Aspler's grandparents). The Pontuses were the Karwasers' landlords, but they lived in another building, and when the situation started to become much worse for Brussels' Jews, the couple offered to take Sylvia in.

Initially, Sylvia's parents hesitated to say yes because of the Pontuses' ages, but they acquiesced when it became clear how dire the situation was.

Within days after Sylvia came to live with the Pontuses, her parents were transported to a transit camp called Caserne Dossin in Malines between Antwerp and Brussels. The vast majority of Belgian Jews sent to Caserne Dossin wound up in Auschwitz, but because of the couple's young ages and ability to work, they lived a full two years there until being liberated by the Allies in 1944.

Also, because the Nazi occupation of Belgium was a bit less severe than elsewhere, Goodman-Aspler said, her grandfather, who worked with leather at the camp, was allowed to briefly go into Brussels, where he visited with his daughter surreptitiously. The visit proved so troubling to little Sylvia, though, that it was decided not to do it again.

After liberation, the family was reunited and they stayed in touch with the Pontuses until their deaths in 1951 and 1952. Sylvia and her parents moved to Toronto in 1955.

Twelve years ago, Goodman-Aspler, herself a veteran of the March of the Living and a psychologist who treats Holocaust survivors and their families, began the effort to

Sylvia Goodman of Toronto, left, and Denise Salmona, the granddaughter of Alida and Charles Pontus, hold the Yad Vashem certificate honouring her grandparents at a ceremony at the Israeli Embassy in Brussels.

Vashem and the Internet bore little fruit.

Then, about two years ago, a cousin of Goodman-Aspler's in the United States, Michal Freedman, who is on the staff of Massachusetts Democratic Congressman Edward Markey, made a personal request to the Belgian embassy for help.

That led to the discovery of a 1942 document listing all the residents of an address in Brussels that included the Pontuses' first names, Alida and Charles.

Incredibly, Goodman-Aspler said, Sylvia Karwaser was among the names listed as living with the Pontuses.

As for someone who could corroborate that the Pontuses had housed Sylvia, that came from Andrée Geulen, a woman credited with saving the lives of more than 1,000 Belgian Jewish children during the war.

"My mother's situation became known to her, and she checked up on her personally," Goodman-Aspler said. "She also had her name in one of four black books she carried with her."

In her speech at the ceremony in Brussels, Goodman-Aspler noted that when her daughter was born in 2002, she was named Nediva, which is Hebrew for "noble," or "generous," in honour of the Pontuses. It was only after finding out the names of Alida Pontus that the family discovered that the names meant the very same thing.

"If it wasn't for their selfless behaviour, we would most likely not be part of this world," Goodman-Aspler said in Brussels. "In this way, the Pontus-

Winnipeg school program

CJN article on Yad Vashem ceremony (January 2007)

Sylvia with close friend, Julia Koschitzky (August 2001)

Sylvia & Osher Goodman

Sylvia & Osher Goodman surrounded by their grandchildren (July 2008)

Sylvia with close friend, Brenda
Freedman , *z'l* (August 2001)

Sylvia with maternal cousin, Michael Hirsh
(May 2010)

Sylvia with Wenner grandchildren at Ami
Wenner's Bar Mitzvah (December 2014)

Sylvia with her children & grandchildren at
Nediva Aspler's Bat Mitzvah (February 2015)

L to R: Sylvia, paternal cousin Chava
Schur, Elana & Sierra Goodman in Israel
(August 2015)

Sylvia with her grandchildren at Gavi Aspler's Bar Mitzvah (June 2017)

L to R: Rachel, Sylvia, Ayala, Noam at Gavi Aspler's Bar Mitzvah (June 2017)

L to R: Shimmy & Ayala Wenner, Rachel & Hudi Aspler, Elana & Noam Goodman at Gavi Aspler's Bar Mitzvah (June 2017)

L to R: Rachel, Noam, Ayala at Gavi
Aspler's Bar Mitzvah (June 2017)

Reunion of Camp Kvutza friends

L to R: Noam & Elana
Goodman, Sylvia Goodman,
Rachel Goodman Aspler, Ayala
Wenner in Israel for Zachary's
Bar Mitzvah (April 2019)

Sylvia in front of the Kotel, eating a green candy for
the 1st time since the war (April 2019)

Sylvia with her Goodman grandchildren at Zachary's Bar
Mitzvah in Israel (April 2019)

Sylvia with her best friends, Ruth Zaretsky
& Hindy Hirt, at her 80th birthday
celebration (May 2019)

L to R: Sylvia, Stephen Freedhoff, Ayala
Wenner, Michal Freedhoff (Sylvia's niece who
helped find the census documents)

Sylvia with her 3 children at her 80th birthday
celebration (May 2019)

Sylvia surrounded by her grandchildren at her 80th
birthday celebration (May 2019)

L to R: Noam & Elana Goodman, Shimmy & Ayala
Wenner, Sylvia Goodman, Rachel & Hudi Aspler, at
Sylvia's 80th birthday celebration (May 2019)

Sylvia with her old school & camp friends at
her 80th birthday celebration (May 2019)

Sylvia with Aspler grandchildren at Talia's Bat
Mitzvah (February 2020)

Acknowledgements

This book is a long time coming, and I only wish that my parents, Getty and Srulek Karwaser, my brother, Willy Karwaser, and my husband, Osher Goodman, could have lived to see its publication.

I do not have sufficient words to thank my parents for their brave decision to put me in the care of the Pontus family, a decision that saved my life, and for their example to live each day to its fullest with deep happiness and joy.

My brother, Willy taught me not to take life too seriously, and to live in the moment.

And to my life partner, Osher, I am deeply appreciative of the wonderful life we lived together building a Jewish home for our children which has filtered down to the next generation and I know will continue for generations to come.

My heartfelt thanks go to several especially important people without whom this book would not have been completed:

To my niece, Michal Freedhoff, whose dedication and persistence with the Belgian Consulate to the United States ensured that we were able to know the full names of all the Pontus' family members. To Michael Hirsh, my cousin, for all his support and encouragement and fact-checking of our family history, and most importantly for his life-long friendship. To Elisa Birnbaum for the hours of work that she put in interviewing me and making sure that my voice was heard within my words. To Miriam Elmaleh and her team at Commerce Press Publishing, for their dedication in bringing this project to its fruition with patience and precision.

And finally, to my children, Noam, Rachel and Ayala and their spouses for encouraging me to share my story with the world and for surrounding me with a loving family for which I am forever grateful.

And, of course, to Alida and Charles Pontus, may their memory be a blessing; we owe our entire existence to them.

www.ingramcontent.com/pod-product-compliance
Lightning Source LLC
Chambersburg PA
CBHW061326120726
48001CB00002B/719